FISH
BIBLE STUDYGUIDES

Ruth

*R*elationships
that bring life

RUTH HALEY BARTON

SHAW BOOKS

an imprint of WATERBROOK PRESS

Ruth

A SHAW BOOK
PUBLISHED BY WATERBROOK PRESS
2375 Telstar Drive, Suite 160
Colorado Springs, Colorado 80920
A division of Random House, Inc.

ISBN 0-87788-865-5

Printed in the United States of America
2002

10 9 8 7 6 5 4 3 2

Contents

How to Use This Studyguide v

Introduction: Relationships That Bring Life 1

1 Don't Let Me Walk This Road Alone 3
   Ruth 1:1-13

2 Love for the Long Haul 9
   Ruth 1:14-22; Psalm 62:5-8

3 Hard Work and Humble Service 15
   Ruth 2:1-23

4 Learning from Each Other 23
   Ruth 3:1-6

5 The Risk of Relationship 29
   Ruth 3:7–4:10

6 The Rewards of Relationship 35
   Ruth 4:11-22

Leader's Notes 41

How to Use This Studyguide

Fisherman studyguides are based on the inductive approach to Bible study. Inductive study is discovery study; we discover what the Bible says as we ask questions about its content and search for answers. This is quite different from the process in which a teacher *tells* a group *about* the Bible—what it means and what to do about it. In inductive study God speaks directly to each of us through his Word.

A group functions best when a leader keeps the discussion on target, but the leader is neither the teacher nor the "answer person." A leader's responsibility is to *ask*—not *tell*. The answers come from the text itself as group members examine, discuss, and think together about the passage.

There are four kinds of questions in each study. The first is an *approach question*. Asked and answered before the Bible passage is read, this question breaks the ice and helps you start thinking about the topic of the Bible study. It begins to reveal where thoughts and feelings need to be transformed by Scripture.

Some of the early questions in each study are *observation questions*—who, what, where, when, and how—designed to help you learn some basic facts about the passage of Scripture.

Once you know what the Bible says, you then need to ask, *What does it mean?* These *interpretation questions* help you to discover the writer's basic message.

Next come *application questions,* which ask, *What does it mean to me?* They challenge you to live out the Scripture's life-transforming message.

Fisherman studyguides provide spaces between questions for jotting down responses as well as any related questions you would like to raise in the group. Each group member should have a copy of the studyguide and may take a turn in leading the group.

A group should use any accurate, modern translation of the Bible such as the *New International Version,* the *New American Standard Bible,* the *New Revised Standard Version,* the *New Jerusalem Bible,* or the *Good News Bible.* (Other translations or paraphrases of the Bible may be referred to when additional help is needed.) Bible commentaries should not be brought to a Bible study because they tend to dampen discussion and keep people from thinking for themselves.

SUGGESTIONS FOR GROUP LEADERS

1. Thoroughly read and study the Bible passage before the meeting. Get a firm grasp on its themes and begin applying its teachings for yourself. Pray that the Holy Spirit will "guide you into all the truth" (John 16:13) so that your leadership will guide others.
2. If any of the studyguide's questions seem ambiguous or unnatural to you, rephrase them, feeling free to add others that seem necessary to bring out the meaning of a verse.
3. Begin (and end) the study promptly. Start by asking someone to pray that every participant will both understand the passage and be open to its transforming power. Remember, the Holy Spirit is the teacher, not you!
4. Ask for volunteers to read the passages aloud.

5. As you ask the studyguide's questions in sequence, encourage everyone to participate in the discussion. If some are silent, try gently suggesting, "Let's have an answer from someone who hasn't spoken up yet."

6. If a question comes up that you can't answer, don't be afraid to admit that you're baffled. Assign the topic as a research project for someone to report on next week, or say, "I'll do some studying and let you know what I find out."

7. Keep the discussion moving, but be sure it stays focused. Though a certain number of tangents are inevitable, you'll want to quickly bring the discussion back to the topic at hand. Also, learn to pace the discussion so that you finish the lesson in the time allotted.

8. Don't be afraid of silences; some questions take time to answer, and some people need time to gather courage to speak. If silence persists, rephrase your question, but resist the temptation to answer it yourself.

9. If someone comes up with an answer that is clearly illogical or unbiblical, ask for further clarification: "What verse suggests that to you?"

10. Discourage overuse of cross references. Learn all you can from the passage at hand, while selectively incorporating a few important references suggested in the studyguide.

11. Some questions are marked with a ✐. This indicates that further information is available in the Leader's Notes at the back of the guide.

12. For further information on getting a new Bible study group started and keeping it functioning effectively, read *You Can Start a Bible Study Group* by Gladys Hunt and *Pilgrims in Progress: Growing Through Groups* by Jim and Carol Plueddemann. (Both books are available from Shaw Books.)

Suggestions for Group Members

1. Learn and apply the following ground rules for effective Bible study. (If new members join the group later, review these guidelines with the whole group.)

2. Remember that your goal is to learn all that you can *from the Bible passage being studied.* Let it speak for itself without using Bible commentaries or other Bible passages. There is more than enough in each assigned passage to keep your group productively occupied for one session. Sticking to the passage saves the group from insecurity ("I don't have the right reference books—or the time to read anything else.") and confusion ("Where did that come from? I thought we were studying _____.").

3. Avoid the temptation to bring up those fascinating tangents that don't really grow out of the passage you are discussing. If the topic is of common interest, you can bring it up later in informal conversation after the study. Meanwhile, help one another stick to the subject.

4. Encourage one another to participate. People remember best what they discover and verbalize for

themselves. Some people are naturally shy, while others may be afraid of making a mistake. If your discussion is free and friendly and you show real interest in what group members think and feel, the quieter ones will be more likely to speak up. Remember, the more people involved in a discussion, the richer it will be.

5. Guard yourself from answering too many questions or talking too much. Give others a chance to share their ideas. If you are one who participates easily, discipline yourself by counting to ten before you open your mouth.

6. Make personal, honest applications and commit yourself to letting God's Word change you.

Relationships That Bring Life

If we desire a more loving society, we individual persons must return to the deepest common sense of our hearts; we must claim love as our true treasure. Then comes the difficult part: we must try to live according to our desire in the moment-by-moment experiences of our lives.

—GERALD MAY

At the heart of human longing is the desire for relationship—for relationships that bring life and love and a sense of belonging. Sometimes that longing stirs when things get quiet around us and we become aware of the solitary nature of human existence. Other times it stirs when we're in a crowd of people, perhaps at a party, where we suddenly realize that although we've done a lot of chatting, we haven't really connected with anyone on a significant level. Sometimes that longing stirs as the credits roll at the end of a movie and we wonder if the kind of love we've just seen on the big screen will ever be ours. And around the holidays, media-generated images of family gatherings might cause a twinge of sadness as we imagine that everyone else's family is happier and more loving than our own.

All of us have moments and even seasons when we are particularly aware of our desire for human relationship. During these times it can be easy to think that if only the people around us would change, they could satisfy our needs. The story of Ruth, however, illustrates the truth that when we stay faithful to our own spiritual journey, we ourselves change and become the kind of people who can bring life to others—even in the midst of very challenging circumstances. As we learn to come alongside others in the ups and downs of life and as we commit ourselves to loving them for the long haul, people will be drawn to us as they sense God's life in us. Then we'll discover that we are able to come together with others in relationships that bring life.

Don't Let Me Walk This Road Alone

RUTH 1:1-13

*God expressed His spirituality by entering into
human relationship, by living and dying as one of
us. He practiced the presence of people by becoming
one Himself. So too each one of us must find a
way to join the human race, casting off our
separateness and throwing in our lot with others.*

—MIKE MASON

The human experience is full of ups and downs. First kisses and championship football games, weddings and births fill us with so much excitement and joy that we feel like bursting. But there are also moments of death and loss and struggle, creating waves of grief that threaten to pull us under.

Tightly packed in the first five verses of the book of Ruth is a sobering, yet matter-of-fact description of some of the highest highs and lowest lows of the human experience. In these very human situations, Ruth's relationships—with God and with others—were forged.

1. Describe a high point and a low point in your life. Who walked with you through those times?

READ RUTH 1:1-5.

✏ 2. What events in the life of this Jewish family are listed in this passage?

3. Which person do you identify with most strongly? Why?

✒ 4. Imagine the events of these five verses from the van-
tage point of the person you just named. What
emotions might he or she have experienced in connection with such life events as famine, poverty,
relocation, weddings, and funerals?

Stress,
Sadness,

5. What kinds of questions and issues do you think
Naomi and her daughters-in-law might have been
wrestling with at the end of verse 5? What do you
think it must have been like for Naomi—a Jewish
woman—to be in a foreign land without her family
of origin and separated from her faith community?

READ RUTH 1:6-13.

6. How does God begin to guide these three women
    who have been through so much together (verses
    6-7)?

7. What is the tone and quality of the relationship
    between this mother-in-law and her daughters-in-
    law (verses 8-13)? What aspects of their relationship
    do you find surprising or unexpected?

8. What diversities are represented in Naomi's relation-
    ships with her daughters-in-law? What made it pos-
    sible for them to journey together despite their
    differences and the difficulties they faced?

9. Why did Naomi try to send Ruth and Orpah back to their own people?

10. What guidance did Naomi offer these young women? What questions did she ask them to consider?

11. What was Naomi's experience and understanding of God at this point in her spiritual journey? What conclusions had she made about God based on her experiences?

12. Think back on the experiences you described in question 1 and the friends who walked with you through the good and the bad times. What did those people do to bring you hope and life? Be specific.

13. What do your own experiences—and the experiences of Naomi, Ruth, and Orpah—teach you about how you can bring hope and life to others by coming alongside them during the highs and lows of the human experience? Who might need you to come alongside them right now?

Love for the Long Haul

RUTH 1:14-22; PSALM 62:5-8

*At times the strength of spiritual community lies
in the love of people who refrain from getting
caught in the trap of trying to fix everything for
us, who pray for us and allow us the pain of
our wilderness, our wants, so that we can
become more deeply grounded in God.*

—ROSEMARY DOUGHERTY

Most of us associate "till death do us part" commitments with wedding ceremonies and marriages. In this study we witness one of the most beautiful expressions of human commitment ever recorded—not in the context of marriage, but in a relationship between two women of different ethnic backgrounds, different faith traditions, and different generations.

In the face of her tragic situation, Naomi was hardly as winsome and optimistic as she might normally have been. Still Ruth stood with her. How life-giving it must have been for Naomi to know that Ruth was committed to love her for the long haul, bearing with her pain without trying to fix her or make things seem better than they were. Friends like Ruth are one of the greatest gifts that life can bring.

1. Who in your life is committed to you for the long haul? When did you begin to recognize the depth of this person's commitment to you? What has this commitment meant to you?

READ RUTH 1:14-18.

2. Why do you think Ruth made such a startling commitment to a woman who, from a human point of view, had nothing to give her? How far did her commitment go?

3. What did Ruth leave behind in order to be with Naomi?

4. Ruth's decision to stay by Naomi's side meant walking away from her past. When have you made a break with some aspect of your past? Describe how hard or easy that step was. What were the results of that decision?

5. Verses 14-18 mark not only Ruth's commitment to Naomi but also her commitment to the one true God. What evidence do you see that Ruth's commitment to Naomi was intertwined with her own spiritual seeking?

READ RUTH 1:19-22.

6.   Why do you think the whole town was "stirred" by the arrival of Naomi and Ruth?

7.   What do Naomi's words in verses 20-21 reveal about the state of her heart and soul? about her awareness of God during these dark days?

8.   When have you felt bitter and dissatisfied with the life God has given you? (You may be feeling that way right now.) With whom did you (or do you) share those feelings? Did (or do) you share them with God? Why or why not?

9. Ruth made a radical commitment to Naomi. How do you think Ruth might have felt when Naomi described her situation as "empty"? In what way(s) did Ruth continue to stand with Naomi even in the darkness of this moment? What restraint did Ruth exercise?

10. What ray of hope does verse 22 offer? Note especially the contrast with the first verse of this chapter.

READ PSALM 62:5-8.

11. Not everything in life can be fixed. In fact, there are times in a person's life when things are so dark that there really is nothing another human being can do except wait with them for God's deliverance. What

insight do the verses from Psalm 62 give us about how to be with ourselves and with others when we face the great unfixables of life?

12. Many of us are more comfortable offering answers and solutions when friends go through hard times than we are with being silent. How easy or difficult is it for you to be with others when all you can do is wait with them for the salvation and deliverance that only God can accomplish? Which of your relationships might need this kind of restraint right now?

Hard Work and Humble Service

Ask any woman who has lost her husband, and she will tell you that a widow's mourning is eventually interrupted by reality. Soon, she is forced to suspend the grieving process long enough to focus her attention on the matter of how she will survive when mourning has passed... It is the persistent love of Ruth's friendship which helped bring about Naomi's healing.

—RENITA WEEMS

I must confess that hard work and humble service are not always my favorite parts of relationships. If left to my most natural inclinations, I would rather have a quiet conversation, take a walk, or attend a family party than take care of people's kids, deliver a meal to someone who is sick, or even return a phone call when I'm tired. But if a relationship lasts long enough, we can be sure that there will be times when bringing life to those we love will involve the hard work of figuring out what they truly need, setting aside our own preferences, and humbly serving in ways that meet their need. But we may also find out, as Ruth did, that the rewards of connecting with God and with others far outweigh any inconveniences and the effort we expend.

1. Describe an unexpected kindness or act of service that you received this past week. How did it bring life to you?

READ RUTH 2:1-17.

2. What very practical matters did Naomi and Ruth need to deal with when they arrived in Bethlehem?

3. What help and encouragement did Ruth and Naomi give each other as they addressed these practical concerns? What character qualities are evident in Ruth's interactions with Naomi and in the way she responds to the need of the moment?

✎ 4. Look again at verses 1-17. During her first day of gleaning, in what ways did Ruth begin to experience God's goodness and his personal care for her? What impact do you think this had on her fledgling relationship with the God of Israel?

5. In this passage we meet Boaz, a man who would play a key role in the lives of Naomi and Ruth. What do we learn about his character, his standing in the community, and his relationship to Naomi?

6. Boaz noticed that Ruth was a newcomer to his fields. When he learned who she was, what did he do to help her? What had Boaz already learned about Ruth?

7. Even in this early stage of their relationship, God used Boaz in Ruth's life as an instrument of his blessing. List the ways Boaz showed kindness and consideration for Ruth even though he hardly knew her.

8. Remember that Ruth was a young widow who was not only new to the Jewish faith but to the community as well. What do you think Boaz's affirmation and kindness meant to her at that particular time in her life? What was Ruth's response to Boaz's kindness?

9. This passage also describes Ruth's early interactions with the Jewish community in Bethlehem—the people she had chosen to be her people by virtue of her commitment to Naomi. What do you notice about the quality of the interactions in this community? What impact would their practice of exchanging words of blessing and showing kindness to the poor have had on people who visited or lived among them? What did their words and actions reflect about the God they served?

10. What do verses 17-18 reveal about Ruth's character?

Note: An *ephah* is about half a bushel or approximately thirty pounds of barley—an unusually generous amount for one day of gleaning.

READ RUTH 2:19-23.

11. Naomi's question in verse 19 gave Ruth the chance to describe her day—and what a day it had been! It had been a day of risk and reward, of hard work and humble service, of kindness given and kindness received. As Ruth reviewed the events of the day, what clear evidence of God's presence and activity in her life would she have seen? At what moments did she bring life to others? When did others bring life to her?

12. What important and encouraging discovery did Naomi make as she listened to Ruth tell about her day of gleaning?

Note: Although Boaz was not a brother to Mahlon, Ruth's deceased husband, he was a close enough relative that he could act as the *kinsman-redeemer*. Jewish law required the brother of a deceased man to marry the widow and father a son in his name. Naomi seemed to sense that Boaz's kindness to Ruth was an expression of his willingness to be a kinsman-redeemer. We will look more closely at the idea of the kinsman-redeemer in the next study.

13. What has chapter 2 taught you about different ways people can bring life to one another? Consider random interactions as well as intentional acts of kindness and words of affirmation. Do you do these kinds of things to bring life to your relationships as much as you (or others!) would like? Is there one relationship in particular that God may be prompting you to be more intentional about bringing life to?

Learning from Each Other

RUTH 3:1-6

*To search for truth is to reach out with our
whole persons for relationships which can re-
form us and the world in the original image of
love. To know the truth is to enter with our
whole persons into relations of mutuality with
the entire creation—relations in which we not
only know, but allow ourselves to be known.*

—PARKER PALMER

One of the blessings of living in relationship with others
is having the opportunity to learn from one another as
we go. If we're willing to pay attention to the wisdom that others have to share, we might spare ourselves from having to
learn *everything* through our own mistakes!

Naomi and Ruth illustrate this kind of learning, and their
example is so remarkable because it involves a mother- and
daughter-in-law from such different backgrounds. Rather than
allowing relational dynamics or ethnic differences to cause her

to close herself off from Naomi's advice, Ruth humbly received the guidance that would one day result in wonderful blessing.

1. Describe a time when you allowed yourself to learn from someone else and were glad that you did.

READ RUTH 3:1-6.

2. Compare and contrast Naomi's perspective at the end of chapter 1 with her perspective at the end of chapter 2 and the beginning of chapter 3. What shift in Naomi's attitude and focus do you notice? What do you think prompted the change?

3. After the crises of famine, death, and relocation had passed, and Ruth and Naomi settled into life in Bethlehem, what concern did Naomi express (verse 1)?

4. One very human element of this Old Testament story that is so easy to miss is the fact that Ruth was a mature adult who found herself single again. Try to identify with Ruth as a single woman who must have asked many of the questions and felt much of the inner turmoil that are often part of this experience. What were some of the struggles that went with being single in Ruth's time and culture? What are some of the struggles that singles experience today?

5. Although it often feels like everyone around us is married, the truth is that all of us have been (or will be) single at one time or another. What questions do times of singleness raise for us? What questions do our times of singleness raise for those who love us? What are some of the most helpful and life-giving ways to address these concerns together?

6. In this passage, Naomi addressed Ruth's marital status directly and proposed a specific course of action. What guidance did Naomi give Ruth?

7. What was Ruth's response to Naomi's wise advice? What made it possible for Ruth to receive Naomi's advice in such a positive way?

8. Ruth was levelheaded about her life situation—she didn't seem to feel the need to push for relationship or to panic about her singleness. Yet at the same time she was willing to take the risks necessary to improve her situation. What do you think enabled Ruth to be like this?

✑ 9. Read Ruth 3:7-18 to learn what happened when Ruth followed Naomi's advice. (We will look at this passage more closely in the next study.) What was the outcome of Ruth's willingness to follow Naomi's guidance? What did Ruth's obedience cause Boaz to recognize about her? (See verse 10.)

10. Are you, like Ruth, able to receive instruction so that you can become wiser? Why or why not? What enables you to receive and act on advice from others? What keeps you from learning from the wisdom of others?

11. Think about the people with whom you are in close
    relationship. Which of these relationships offer you
    the opportunity to learn from someone and to
    increase in wisdom? How can you become even
    more intentional about learning from these people?

The Risk of Relationship

RUTH 3:7–4:10

*We probably have wondered in our many
lonesome moments if there is one corner in this
competitive, demanding world where it is safe
to be released, to expose ourselves to someone
else, and to give unconditionally. It might be
very small and hidden. But if this corner exists,
it calls for a search through the complexities of
our human relationships in order to find it.*

—HENRI NOUWEN

I still remember one of the first times someone betrayed my trust. During my freshman year in college I dated a guy who was a spiritual leader at the small Bible college we attended. I liked him a lot, and he seemed to be trustworthy. Imagine my shock and pain when I discovered that he was dating two women at the same time, after leading us both to believe that our relationship with him was exclusive. When confronted, he acknowledged what he had done, but that did little to ease the pain or undo the disillusionment he had caused.

Let's face it: Relationships can be very risky—especially when we choose to open our heart and entrust it to another person.

1. What are some of the risks we take when we choose to open our heart to someone?

READ RUTH 3:7-18.

2. Learning to trust people involves deepening our trust in God—in his goodness, in his ability to care for us, and in his presence in the person we are feeling led to trust. What evidence have you seen that Ruth's and Naomi's trust in God was growing and deepening? Why would their growing trust in God have enabled them to trust others?

✒ 3. Up to this point, the story has been primarily
       about Naomi and Ruth, but now Boaz takes
       center stage in this unfolding drama. What have
       you already learned about Boaz, his life, and his
       character?

  4. How did Boaz demonstrate that he could be
      trusted?

✒ 5. Although Hebrew customs may seem strange to us,
       the Bible gives us a real-life account of courtship that
       led to marriage between two individuals who, for
       different reasons, had probably given up on the idea
       of getting married. At that time, as now, it undoubt-
       edly would have seemed quite difficult, if not impos-
       sible, for either Ruth or Boaz to find Mr. or Miss
       Right. Looking back over studies 2, 3, and 4, what
       observations can you make about the beginning of

their relationship and their developing courtship?
What qualities did Ruth and Boaz notice and value
in one another?

6. What risks did Ruth and Boaz take as they opened
   their hearts to each other? What words or actions
   revealed their wisdom and restraint regarding the
   timetable for their relationship?

7. How did Ruth and Boaz benefit from honoring the
   wisdom of others and the traditions of their community? What did Naomi say in verse 18 to encour-

age Ruth to trust both God and Boaz? Why do you think Ruth listened?

8. In what ways did their individual relationships with God shape Boaz's and Ruth's responses to each other? At what point do you sense they knew they could trust each other with their hearts and lives?

READ RUTH 4:1-10.

9. What did Boaz do to follow through on the commitment he made to Ruth? What was his strategy?

10. Why did the closest kinsman refuse his right to redeem Elimelech's possessions?

11. What might Ruth have been thinking and feeling as Boaz and the elders of the city were deciding her fate? What kind of faith do you need in order to allow someone else to represent your interests, especially when the stakes are high?

12. In what current relationship, if any, do you sense that God is leading you to greater levels of trust—in him, in the other person, or both? What will you do to follow his lead?

The Rewards of Relationship

RUTH 4:11-22

Do not fear...I will pour my Spirit upon your
descendants, and my blessing upon your
offspring. They shall spring up like a green
tamarisk, like willows by flowing streams.

—ISAIAH 44:2-4

For me, one of life's most precious gifts is rich and ongoing relationships with members of my extended family—with my parents, my brothers and sisters, their spouses, and their children. Over the years as our family has grown, we have worked hard to maintain authentic relationships with each other. At times certain relationships have been difficult and we've been tempted to walk away from each other. But we've chosen to keep growing in our abilities to give and receive truth from one another, to work through our differences, to learn how to communicate value and love, and, most of all, to remain deeply committed to one another over the long haul.

What we are noticing now is that those years of hard work

have paid off in relationships that are life-giving not only for ourselves but also for the next generation. Our children are finally starting to appreciate what a treasure this community of fellow travelers is, and within this circle they are making their own faith journeys. Together we are learning that, as risky as relationships can be and as much hard work as they can require, life offers nothing quite so satisfying as relationships that have grown in love and trust and greater commitment. Such relationships bring life not only to the people involved but also to those around them.

1. Describe one relationship that, over time, has grown in love and trust and greater commitment. What are some of the blessings you've received from that relationship? What blessings have people outside the relationship experienced because of it?

READ RUTH 4:11-12.

2. Although we tend to consider our intimate relationships a private matter, the story of Ruth and Boaz demonstrates some of the benefits of allowing our relationships to unfold and take shape openly in the larger community of faith. What blessing did Boaz

and Ruth receive from their community as they moved into committed relationship with each other?

✑ 3. How do you think it might have blessed Ruth to know that the Jewish community was praying that God would make her "like Rachel and Leah, who together built the house of Israel"?

READ RUTH 4:13-22.

4. Verse 13 captures in just a few words the dramatic climax to the book of Ruth. Think about how much human emotion is contained in the short sentence "So Boaz took Ruth and she became his wife"! Remembering what Naomi, Ruth, and Boaz had been through, imagine what this event must have meant to each one of them. What thoughts and feelings do you think they might have expressed to God on that day?

5. What does this verse tell us about God's involvement in the process of conception and birth? (Remember that Ruth had remained childless during her ten years of marriage to her first husband.)

6. What did the women of Bethlehem do to help celebrate God's goodness to Naomi?

7. What spiritual lessons did the women of Bethlehem highlight in their blessing?

8. Compare the women's comments about Ruth (verse 15) with the sentiments Naomi expressed when she first returned to Bethlehem (1:20-21). What different perspective did the women offer?

9. Why was the birth of Obed further evidence of God's goodness not only to Ruth but also to Naomi?

10. When we think about several generations in a family trying to live together, we tend to picture a situation that is difficult or even impossible. What details suggest that such was not the case for Naomi, Boaz, Ruth, and baby Obed?

11. What does the brief genealogy in verses 18-22 reveal about the goodness with which God blessed future generations because a few individuals were faithful to each other and to God's call on their lives? (See also Matthew 1:1-17.) What is the significance of the fact that Christ descended from the line of Ruth and Boaz?

12. One of things that is so striking about Ruth is that she brought life and goodness to everyone she touched—whether Naomi, the townspeople, Boaz, or future generations who received a godly heritage that culminated in the birth of Jesus Christ. Which people in your life do you feel called to be in relationship with for the long haul, just as Ruth was called to be with Naomi, Boaz, and the Bethlehem community for the long haul? What can you do to become more intentional about bringing life to those people?

As you end this study, take a few minutes to write a prayer that reflects your desire to be one who brings life to others.

Leader's Notes

STUDY 1: DON'T LET ME WALK THIS ROAD ALONE

Question 2. Ruth lived during the period of the judges, a time of darkness and apostasy in Israel's history when "all the people did what was right in their own eyes" (Judges 21:25). Ruth, however, was not an Israelite. She was of Moabite ancestry. Moab was the nation that issued from Lot's incestuous relationship with his eldest daughter; it was a nation that often warred against Israel. The fact that an Israelite family chose to live among the Moabites gives us some sense of the desperation they felt. This account of Ruth's life provides us with a refreshing reminder that even in the darkest times and in the most unlikely situations, God is still at work calling out beauty, commitment, and purpose.

Question 4. Because the biblical narrative is so brief, we can easily miss the significance and the life-shaping nature of these events. It is also easy for us to distance ourselves from the humanness of biblical characters because they lived so long ago and in such different historical settings. To help your group members fully engage with this story and God's activity in it, allow them time to imagine themselves in the situation this family found itself in. Encourage your group to think about how people experience these kinds of events.

Question 10. In verse 11 Naomi expressed her concern about her daughters-in-law being able to marry again. In the ancient

Near East a woman without a husband was in a serious situation because she lacked security. Naomi referred to the levirate custom in Israel in which a brother was responsible to marry his deceased brother's wife in order to conceive a son and perpetuate his brother's name and inheritance. Naomi pointed out that this law wouldn't help Ruth and Orpah since she had no more sons and was past childbearing age.

STUDY 2: LOVE FOR THE LONG HAUL

Question 5. Besides revealing her commitment to Naomi, Ruth's words indicate that she was a spiritual seeker who was in the process of crossing the line of faith in the one true God, the God Naomi knew. Each of us crosses that line when we first acknowledge that our deepest need is relationship with God, but our sinfulness has separated us from him and from the abundant life he wants for us. We take the second step when we accept by faith that God's Son, Jesus Christ, is the one who reconciled us to God by taking the punishment for our sins so that we can live a new life in the power of his Spirit. As we experience authentic transformation in life-giving connection to God, we will be able to offer life-giving relationships to others.

Maybe someone has been a Naomi to you, pointing you to God in the everyday events of life. If you have questions about faith in God and what it means to name Jesus as your Savior and Lord, ask that person whose example you've noticed. Or perhaps God is using you as a Naomi in someone's life right now. Ask God to show you how you can help that person cross the line into faith.

Question 7. Naomi means "sweetness" or "pleasantness." *Mara,* which means "bitter," seemed to more accurately capture Naomi's sense of herself at this time. Notice that no one seemed to take her up on her desire to be called by this name!

Questions 11-12. Those of us who have faced our own unfixables understand the significance of having friends who can be with us without trying to fix things or offer easy answers that only trivialize the depths of our pain. At a conference on Spiritual Formation at Trinity Evangelical Divinity School (June 17, 1999), I heard Christian author and psychologist Larry Crabb say, "I don't believe we are involved in each other's spiritual formation until we have entered into each other's lives to the point of feeling profoundly inadequate—and not fighting it." When we are able to be with others in the midst of their pain, and when we wait with them in God's presence in silent expectation for him to respond, then we honor the depth of their life experience and acknowledge the reality that God alone can heal their bitterness and pain.

STUDY 3: HARD WORK AND HUMBLE SERVICE

Question 4. Jewish custom provided for the poor by protecting their rights to gather grain in a field after the hired workers had passed through. The edges of the field were to be left for the poor to reap (Leviticus 19:9-10; 23:22).

Question 7. One of the key words in the book of Ruth is the word *hesed,* which means "loyalty borne out of love and kindness toward those to whom a person is responsible." (Definition taken from *The Bible Knowledge Commentary* by John Walvoord and Roy Zuck, Chariot Victor, 1987.) This concept is a unifying thread throughout the book. Naomi asked God to show his kindness to her daughters-in-law (1:8), and she spoke of the kindness he showed them through Boaz (2:20). Ruth spoke of Boaz's *hesed* to her (2:13), and Boaz later affirmed this same quality in Ruth, relative to her choice to marry him instead of a younger man (3:10).

Question 8. Given the fact that Naomi had not yet been able to acknowledge the gift that Ruth had been to her, it may have meant a great deal to Ruth to know that someone had noticed her heart and been so generous and kind to her. What healing this must have brought to her soul!

STUDY 4: LEARNING FROM EACH OTHER

Question 3. While Naomi's involvement in Ruth's love life might be regarded as unwelcome meddling in our culture, it was customary for Hebrew parents to arrange marriages for their children.

Question 6. To our way of thinking, Naomi's plan seems, at best, a bit strange or forward. At worst, we might worry that Naomi's plan would have endangered Ruth by leaving her open to sexual advances, but there is nothing in the passage to support that concern. Rather, Naomi's advice seems to indicate her deep respect both for Boaz and for his position as a potential kinsman-redeemer.

As noted in study 3, according to Jewish law, when a husband died without offspring, the nearest brother-in-law could be called upon to marry the widow and father a son who would assume the family name of his dead brother. In Ruth's case, there was no brother-in-law, so the nearest of kin could be called upon to act as a redeemer. Ruth's request that Boaz spread his garment over her symbolized her desire for him to become her kinsman-redeemer. This request placed her in a very vulnerable position, in which, at the very least, she risked personal rejection.

Question 7. Titus 2:1-7 clearly sets forth the principle of older women and men offering wise counsel to younger women and men. Such learning from another generation can, however, present challenges. Younger men and women might need to humble themselves and admit that they don't have all the answers. More mature men and women might need to be careful to communicate an open and nonjudgmental attitude in response to the questions and ideas of younger generations. If we are aware of what keeps us from learning from one another, we can choose to have a teachable spirit. That position of humility will enable us to receive all that God wants to give us through the people that he has placed in our lives and to give to them what he has for us to share.

Question 9. Ruth is an excellent example of a person who was able to learn from the wisdom of others, especially from someone who had lived more life than she had. Coming from Moab, Ruth was unfamiliar with Jewish custom and could not have known how to proceed in her situation. Her willingness to follow Naomi's wise counsel even though it must have

seemed strange to her illustrates the truth of Proverbs 9:9—
"Give instruction to the wise, and they will become wiser still;
teach the righteous and they will gain in learning."

STUDY 5: THE RISK OF RELATIONSHIP

Question 3. The portrayal of Boaz as Ruth's kinsman-redeemer
is one of Scripture's beautiful illustrations of the Lord Jesus
Christ, kinsman-redeemer for the human race. Jesus purchased
us with his blood, thereby providing us with the peace and
security that come from knowing that we belong to him eter-
nally. Boaz's trustworthy response to Ruth's situation foreshad-
ows the trustworthy nature of Christ's commitment to us.

Question 5. Although the Hebrew concept of kinsman-
redeemer seems somewhat strange to us, Boaz and Ruth dealt
with some of the same issues we moderns do as relationships
unfold. They observed each other from a distance and slowly
began to get acquainted. Both parties needed to find ways to
express their willingness to explore the relationship's possibili-
ties. Boaz and Ruth also had to face issues like communication,
growing trust, eventual commitment, and planning for the
future.

Question 10. The nearer kinsman may have feared that if Ruth
bore him a son, that son would eventually inherit not only the
redeemed property but, in all likelihood, part of his own estate
as well. He probably did not want to endanger his own children's inheritance. By first offering the land and then revealing
that the deal would include marrying Ruth, Boaz may have
been trying to establish that, although the nearer kinsman

might have been willing to acquire more land, he had no real interest in continuing the line of Elimelech.

STUDY 6: THE REWARDS OF RELATIONSHIP

Question 3. Rachel and Leah were Jacob's wives, and they became the mothers of the twelve tribes of Israel. Their story begins in Genesis 29.

Question 9. According to the Hebrew custom of kinsman-redeemer, Naomi could have become the wife of Boaz had she not been past childbearing years. Given Naomi's age, the only way to continue the family line was to have children in the name of Mahlon, Naomi's deceased son. Verses 16-17 may or may not indicate a formal adoption. The point is that Naomi's family line would now continue, and that was a great blessing given the cultural values of that day.

Question 11. Ruth was one of only four women named in the genealogy of Christ, and she was the only non-Jew.

What Should We Study Next?

To help your group answer that question, we've listed the Fisherman studyguides by category so you can choose your next study.

TOPICAL STUDIES

Angels by Vinita Hampton Wright

Becoming Women of Purpose by Ruth Haley Barton

Building Your House on the Lord: Marriage and Parenthood by Steve and Dee Brestin

The Creative Heart of God: Living with Imagination by Ruth Goring

Discipleship: The Growing Christian's Lifestyle by James and Martha Reapsome

Doing Justice, Showing Mercy: Christian Actions in Today's World by Vinita Hampton Wright

Encouraging Others: Biblical Models for Caring by Lin Johnson

The End Times: Discovering What the Bible Says by E. Michael Rusten

Examining the Claims of Jesus by Dee Brestin

Friendship: Portraits in God's Family Album by Steve and Dee Brestin

The Fruit of the Spirit: Growing in Christian Character by Stuart Briscoe

Great Doctrines of the Bible by Stephen Board

Great Passages of the Bible by Carol Plueddemann

Great Prayers of the Bible by Carol Plueddemann

Growing Through Life's Challenges by James and Martha Reapsome

Guidance & God's Will by Tom and Joan Stark

Heart Renewal: Finding Spiritual Refreshment by Ruth Goring

Higher Ground: Steps Toward Christian Maturity by Steve and Dee Brestin

Images of Redemption: God's Unfolding Plan Through the Bible by Ruth Van Reken

Integrity: Character from the Inside Out by Ted Engstrom and Robert Larson

Lifestyle Priorities by John White

Marriage: Learning from Couples in Scripture by R. Paul and Gail Stevens

Miracles by Robbie Castleman

One Body, One Spirit: Building Relationships in the Church by Dale and Sandy Larsen

The Parables of Jesus by Gladys Hunt

Parenting with Purpose and Grace by Alice Fryling

Prayer: Discovering What the Bible Says by Timothy Jones and Jill Zook-Jones

The Prophets: God's Truth Tellers by Vinita Hampton Wright

Proverbs and Parables: God's Wisdom for Living by Dee Brestin

Satisfying Work: Christian Living from Nine to Five by R. Paul Stevens and Gerry Schoberg

Senior Saints: Growing Older in God's Family by James and Martha Reapsome

The Sermon on the Mount: The God Who Understands Me
     by Gladys Hunt
Spiritual Gifts by Karen Dockrey
Spiritual Hunger: Filling Your Deepest Longings by Jim and
     Carol Plueddemann
A Spiritual Legacy: Faith for the Next Generation by Chuck
     and Winnie Christensen
Spiritual Warfare by A. Scott Moreau
The Ten Commandments: God's Rules for Living by Stuart
     Briscoe
Ultimate Hope for Changing Times by Dale and Sandy
     Larsen
Who Is God? by David P. Seemuth
Who Is Jesus? In His Own Words by Ruth Van Reken
Who Is the Holy Spirit? by Barbara Knuckles and Ruth Van
     Reken
Wisdom for Today's Woman: Insights from Esther by Poppy
     Smith
Witnesses to All the World: God's Heart for the Nations
     by Jim and Carol Plueddemann
Women at Midlife: Embracing the Challenges by Jeanie
     Miley
Worship: Discovering What Scripture Says by Larry Sibley

BIBLE BOOK STUDIES

Genesis: Walking with God by Margaret Fromer and
     Sharrel Keyes
Exodus: God Our Deliverer by Dale and Sandy Larsen
Ezra and Nehemiah: A Time to Rebuild by James Reapsome

(For Esther, see Topical Studies, *Wisdom for Today's Woman*)

Job: Trusting Through Trials by Ron Klug

Psalms: A Guide to Prayer and Praise by Ron Klug

Proverbs: Wisdom That Works by Vinita Hampton Wright

Ecclesiastes: A Time for Everything by Stephen Board

Jeremiah: The Man and His Message by James Reapsome

Jonah, Habakkuk, and Malachi: Living Responsibly
by Margaret Fromer and Sharrel Keyes

Matthew: People of the Kingdom by Larry Sibley

Mark: God in Action by Chuck and Winnie Christensen

Luke: Following Jesus by Sharrel Keyes

John: The Living Word by Whitney Kuniholm

Acts 1–12: God Moves in the Early Church by Chuck and
Winnie Christensen

Acts 13–28, see *Paul* under Character Studies

Romans: The Christian Story by James Reapsome

1 Corinthians: Problems and Solutions in a Growing Church
by Charles and Ann Hummel

Strengthened to Serve: 2 Corinthians by Jim and Carol
Plueddemann

Galatians, Titus, and Philemon: Freedom in Christ
by Whitney Kuniholm

Ephesians: Living in God's Household by Robert Baylis

Philippians: God's Guide to Joy by Ron Klug

Colossians: Focus on Christ by Luci Shaw

Letters to the Thessalonians by Margaret Fromer and
Sharrel Keyes

Letters to Timothy: Discipleship in Action by Margaret
Fromer and Sharrel Keyes

Hebrews: Foundations for Faith by Gladys Hunt

James: Faith in Action by Chuck and Winnie Christensen

1 and 2 Peter, Jude: Called for a Purpose by Steve and Dee
    Brestin
How Should a Christian Live? 1, 2, and 3 John by Dee
    Brestin
Revelation: The Lamb Who Is a Lion by Gladys Hunt

BIBLE CHARACTER STUDIES

Abraham: Model of Faith by James Reapsome
David: Man After God's Own Heart by Robbie Castleman
Elijah: Obedience in a Threatening World by Robbie
    Castleman
Great People of the Bible by Carol Plueddemann
King David: Trusting God for a Lifetime by Robbie
    Castleman
Men Like Us: Ordinary Men, Extraordinary God by Paul
    Heidebrecht and Ted Scheuermann
Moses: Encountering God by Greg Asimakoupoulos
Paul: Thirteenth Apostle (Acts 13–28) by Chuck and
    Winnie Christensen
Women Like Us: Wisdom for Today's Issues by Ruth Haley
    Barton
Women Who Achieved for God by Winnie Christensen
Women Who Believed God by Winnie Christensen

About the Author

Ruth Haley Barton is a graduate of Wheaton College and was trained as a spiritual director at the Shalem Institute for Spiritual Direction in Washington, D.C. Ruth is a wife and a mother of three daughters (ages 11, 16, and 18) as well as an author and speaker. Her published works include *Equal to the Task: Men and Women in Partnership, Becoming a Woman of Strength,* and three Fisherman Bible Studyguides. Formerly the associate director of spiritual formation at Willow Creek Community Church, Ruth coauthored (with John Ortberg) *An Ordinary Day with Jesus: Experiencing the Reality of God in Your Everyday Life* and contributed to *The Couples' Devotional Bible* and *Today's Christian Woman Study Bible.*